WHOSE IMAGE AND WHICH MIND

Greg Violi

D1248697

OVERCOMER

WHOSE IMAGE AND WHICH MIND
Copyright © 2012 by Greg Violi. All rights reserved.

Published by OVERCOMER, Lintheide 11, 33719 Bielefeld, Germany.
Book design copyright © 2012 by OVERCOMER. All rights reserved.

For more information about the author and this message please visit this website: www.aplaceforhisglory.com. There you can also contact and invite Greg Violi to your place. You can also find videos and sermons from Greg Violi on www.erweckt.de with different translations.

Contents

Introductory Remarks

This small booklet will discuss the mystery of godliness and the mystery of iniquity and the mind that has wisdom and the carnal mind with its corrupted, defiled wisdom of satan!

"And here is the mind which hath wisdom"

Revelation 17:9a

*"For the **mystery of lawlessness** (that hidden principle of rebellion against constituted authority) is already at work in the world, [but it is] restrained only until he who restrains is taken out of the way."*

2 Thessalonians 2:7

*"And without controversy great is the **mystery of godliness**: God was manifest in the flesh, justified in the Spirit, seen of angels, preached unto the Gentiles, believed on in the world, received up into glory."*

1 Timothy 3:16

"For to be carnally minded is death; but to be spiritually minded is life and peace. Because the carnal mind is enmity against God: for it is not subject to the law of God, neither indeed can be."

Romans 8:6-7

"Thine heart was lifted up because of thy beauty, thou hast corrupted thy wisdom by reason of thy brightness: I will cast thee to the ground, I will lay thee before kings, that they may behold thee."

Ezekiel 28:17

We will study the spiritual heart that we are born with and the corrupted wisdom or foolishness that every child receives at birth. We will investigate the nature of this natural heart and then study the *Heavenly Wisdom* and the heart of the Lamb. Lastly, we will discover the splendor of living life in the heart of the Lamb and being fed from the river of divine wisdom! Each heart has a source from which its wisdom flows. Even a Christian can be feeding from the wrong source of wisdom. Therefore, this booklet is of vital importance for this hour!

The Serpent's Poison becomes Man's Pride

Satan was created perfect and his heart was blameless until iniquity was found in him. Every created being is dependent and derives all of its sustenance from the One who created it. In Him we have our being, we move and we live (Acts 17:28). When someone starts to look at itself as an independent entity, they are now a *god* in their own mind. This is the main reason that satan´s heart was lifted up on the inside. He saw himself as an independent entity, one with equal power and beauty and glory as his Creator. In his own mind, he did not require or need a God, for he was sufficient in himself to rule his own life. Now, since he was sufficient to rule his life, he could also rule the lives of others. This is how a "*god*" thinks and now they know what is good for themselves and others as well. This is how satan became the devil and his heart was filled with a wicked substance called pride or self exaltation. Satan tempted the pure and holy Son of God with the same temptation.

Jesus came as a perfect man. He was both God and man, but, since God cannot be tempted (James 1:13b), then Jesus Christ had to overcome all temptations as a perfect man. He was tempted in all points as we are (Heb. 4:15), and therefore he had to demonstrate what a perfect man looks like. A perfect man is totally dependent on its Creator for all things and he can do not one thing out of himself (John 5:19, 30). Satan tried to tempt Jesus to do something out of himself, like "turn these stones into bread, if you are the son of God!" Jesus was constantly refusing to do anything out of himself, but he constantly chose to do all things out of his father. He even said that if he spoke out of himself, then he would be seeking his own glory! This is the literal meaning of John 7:18.

"Before destruction, the heart of man is haughty and before honor is humility."

Proverbs 18:12

The five defects of man's heart at birth

Defect 1: A wrong attitude that one can, of *his own self and ability*, succeed and climb the ladder of life. Example: a better job, a better marriage, a bigger house, a bigger and better ministry, and get to heaven.

Defect 2: A wrong attitude that says *"I must be number one"*. I must win the game, the contest. I must achieve the highest grade in school. I must "outdo" all the other competitors no matter what the field of life (entertainment, sports, glamour, finances, ministry, education etc.). Doing my best is not sufficient. I must *be* the very best. This defective attitude creates a perfect environment for the viruses of jealousy, self condemnation, envy, and suspicion to grow. This in turn will open the door to confusion and every evil thing (James 3:16).

Defect 3: A wrong attitude that tells me I *deserve to be noticed.* This attitude drives a person to get attention; whether they have earned it or not. They are simply driven from the inside to receive attention, especially if another which they deem less worthy than themselves is receiving it. This person will even discredit the name of another so that he might receive more honor and recognition for himself. This attitude creates an unconscious need to be seen in the limelight. When this person is not noticed it will cause them to be offended.

Defect 4: A wrong attitude that teaches one that it is ok to live *outside the circle of responsibility.* One thinks, "as long as I have a feeling of well-being and peace, I do not need to ponder any unmet needs or debts or obligations." This false attitude will cause one to lose his conscious awareness of earthly chores and responsibilities. Living where the soil is dirty does not appeal to this one. This one will avoid tasks like scrubbing toilets and changing diapers. "Others can do those things, I have more important things to do" this one thinks. Their soul is communicating to them the thought, "Flee as a bird to your mountain" (Psalms11:1). Unfortunately, this thought is more appealing than the thought of dealing with earthly matters.

Sometimes the deceiver will trick this dear one into thinking that his visionary experiences (above the heights of the clouds) are from God, but they might be from the evil one. Sometimes we fear earthly responsibilities because of hidden issues of the soul. The earthly responsibilities can cause a person that has many fears to avoid the need to make a decision all together.

Defect 5: The worst of all the heart defects is the one that convinces a person that they need no help from either man or God. This faulty attitude says, *"I am as god and therefore should be treated with reverence and* *appreciation as God would receive."* This erroneous attitude convinces a person that what they feel and believe has to be correct, and all rebukes and admonitions are unjust and undeserved. This one believes that the real problem is with *others*. So, in effect, this horrible attitude convinces one that they do not need others, but *others need them!* Many offenses are stirred up within this attitude of the heart, simply due to the fact that others do not give the due respect (phone call, invitation, hug, letter, hand shake) that this one feels he deserves.

How did these defects come inside of man?

Man received the spirit or breath of the serpent in the garden. The evil one, through the instrumentality of the serpent, accused God and told man that they would be like God. After receiving these words from the heart of the liar, then their nature underwent a change and their very DNA was poisoned. Man was created in the image and nature of God (Genesis 1:26), but Adam had a son in his own image (Genesis 5:3). This image had a fallen nature (1 Corinthians 15:49).

Paul said that all men are by nature under the wrath of God (Ephesians 2:3) and this nature desires the lusts of the flesh and the lustful, selfish thoughts of the mind. Isaiah said that we all go our own way (Isaiah 53:6). Jeremiah said, *"The heart is deceitful and desperately wicked"* (Jeremiah 17:9). Jesus said, *"You generation of vipers* (serpents), *how can you, being evil, speak good things? For out of the abundance of the heart the mouth speaks"* (Matthew 12:34). John said that the whole world lies in the evil one and his power (1 John5:19). Solomon said that every man's way is right in his own eyes (Proverbs 21:2).

The Bible describes man's nature as sinful (1 John 1:8). The flesh is the sin nature. The mind of flesh has an internal hatred of God and all that He loves. The heart is desperately wicked by nature because of one reason only: it has set itself (self) on the throne and taken God (True Sovereign) off the throne of the heart. This occurred in the Garden of Eden. Ever since the fall, *self* has refused to give the throne back to the *true* Ruler. This is why Jesus said the first requirement to receive Him is to deny self (Matthew 16:24, Luke 9:23).

Another description of this selfish, wicked heart is the image of the beast. This heart is lifted up on the inside and full of selfishness. Out of this lifted up heart proceeds a substance that God hates called *pride*. When a heart gets lifted up, the first thing to come out of it is pride. This poison is a wicked venom that will always cause harm to others.

On the other hand, when a heart is bowed down on the inside, the first thing to come out of it is the substance of Christ's own heart, which is *humility* (Matthew 11:29). It is out of the attitude of lowliness and humility that the Lord can then create true worshippers. David said come let us bow down and worship (Psalm 95:6). King Nebuchadnezzar was judged for one thing: a heart that was lifted up on the inside (Daniel 4:16). In Habakkuk 2:4 it says when a living, breathing creature is lifted up on the inside, he is not upright. To be upright is to have a right posture of humility that receives all from their Creator to be in and do through a person. Mankind was never intended to have a heart lifted up in pride. This is the image of another, and this image will be worshipped by many in the last days. It declares in the book of Revelation that many will even curse God and die after His judgments on them. This is how pride will always deal with personal criticism. They will not tolerate any idea that they deserve to be judged. In their own eyes they are always right. What is in a person's heart is the essence of that person. For "*as a man thinketh within his heart, so is he*" (Proverbs 23:7a). The heart of the serpent, beast or evil one is fully described for us in Isaiah 14:12-15. Lucifer spoke five "I wills" within his heart:

"For thou hast said in thine heart, "I will ascend to heaven; I will exalt my throne above the stars of God; I will sit also upon the mount of the congregation, in the sides of the north; I will ascend above the heights of the clouds; I will be like the Most High."

Isaiah 14:13-14

Each of these is parallel to the five heart defects of the *human* spiritual heart:

Defect 1: *"I will ascend into the heaven"*

A wrong attitude that one can, of his own ability, succeed and climb the ladder of success in this life and the next.

Defect 2: *"I will exalt my throne above the stars of God"*

A wrong attitude that says that I must be number one, the very best.

Defect 3: *"I will sit also upon the mount of the congregation in the sides of the north"*

A wrong attitude that tells me that I deserve to be noticed. I must have the attention. Psalm 48:2 says, *"Beautiful for situation, the joy of the whole earth, is Mount Zion, on the sides of the north, the city of the great King"*. This speaks of the place of honor that God chooses to bestow on some. Remember before honor comes humility (Proverbs 18:12).

Defect 4: *"I will ascend above the heights of the clouds"*

An attitude that teaches one that it is "ok" to live outside the circle of responsibility. Above the heights of the clouds is above the earth with all of it's responsibilities.

Defect 5: *"I will be as the Most High"*

This attitude convinces one that they need no help from either man or God. It also declares, "I am needed but I do not need you". Now this wicked heart must be destroyed within a people, especially in the last days! How do we overcome this wicked heart?

The Honored Heart of the Lamb

The Lamb's heart, or the mystery of godliness (Christ revealed in the flesh) is the way to overcome the mystery of iniquity (Satan revealed in the flesh). We joyously discover five "I wills" within the heart of the Lamb of God revealed in Philippians 2:6-8. The word that Paul uses for the "mind" in chapter two of Philippians is actually referring to the attitude of one's heart.

> *"Who being in the form of God, thought it not robbery to be equal with God: but made himself of no reputation, and took upon him the form of a servant, and was made in the likeliness of men: and being found in fashion as a man, he humbled himself, and became obedient unto death, even the death of the cross."*
>
> Philippians 2:6-8

Attitude 1: *"Who being in the form of God thought it not robbery to be equal to God"*

The first attitude of the heart of Christ was: *I will* not esteem who I am and what I deserve.

Attitude 2: "He was made in the likeness of men"

The second attitude of heart says: *I will* lower myself and become identified with the transgressors in their failures, weaknesses and deep seated issues of heart (Hebrews 2:16-18, Isaiah 53:12b).

Attitude 3: "He made himself of no reputation"

The third attitude of the Lamb's heart was: I will become nothing in the minds of others around me. Reputation describes how a person is seen in man's eyes. All mankind lives for their reputation, but Jesus made himself of no reputation. He would not allow any thoughts that another human being had towards him affect him in any way. He only sought the approval of One.

Attitude 4: "He took upon him the form of a servant"

This fourth attitude of heart says: I will take the outward appearance of a slave and receive the scorn and ridicule that might come from others. This attitude causes one to take the outward form of a servant – and all mankind looks at the outward appearance of a person (I Samuel 16:7a). This will surely cause the critical ones to scorn and despise you simply because of your dress and mannerisms. Servants are not esteemed in any society or culture. It is good to recall one of Jesus' teachings at this point. *"That which is highly esteemed among men is an abomination in the sight of God"* (Luke 16:15b).

16

Attitude 5: *"Being found in fashion as a man he humbled himself and became obedient unto death, even the death of the cross"*

This attitude of heart says: I will set my face like a flint all my life to obey my Father God and receive His approval, no matter what the world might say about me, or do to me. This is the greatest attitude of the Lamb of God. This attitude is a total determination to obey God no matter what the consequences might be. This included dying the most despicable type of death for a Jewish person to die: a crucifixion on a cross. This also includes being wrongfully judged, especially by the ones that should have known you the best, your own people. Any Israelite would have known that their Scriptures taught that someone who hangs on a tree is cursed by God (Deuteronomy 21:23). It is one thing to give your life, but it must be much harder when the ones you love, and are dying for, are laughing you to scorn even while you are hanging on a cross in excruciating pain (Psalm 22:7-8).

The Lamb of God started in the highest place (equal with God) and then by five *"I wills"* took the very lowest place, dying the death of a slave cursed by God. The result of this course of action is found in Philippians 2:9-11:

> *"Wherefore, God also hath highly exalted Him and given Him the name which is above every name. That at the name of Jesus every knee shall bow, of things in heaven, and things in earth, and things under the earth; and that every tongue should confess that Jesus Christ is Lord, to the glory of God the Father."*

The other heart, the serpent heart of Lucifer tried to climb higher and higher until he declares, "I will be as the Most High," and what is the outcome of this one? Isaiah 14:15 tells us, *"Yet thou shall be brought down to hell, to the sides of the pit."*

Summary

The Haughty, despised heart of Lucifer (Isaiah 14:13)

1. I will ascend to heaven.

2. I will exalt my throne above the other stars of God

3. I will sit also in the mount of the congregation, in the sides of the north

4. I will ascend above the heights of the clouds

5. I will be as the Most High

The Lowly, honored heart of the Lamb (Philippians 2:6-11)

1. I will not esteem who I really am and what I really deserve

2. I will lower myself and be identified with transgressors in their failures, weaknesses, and deep issues and pains of their hearts.

3. I will become nothing in the minds of others. No reputation.

4. I will take the outward appearance of a slave and receive the scorn and ridicule that might come from others.

5. I will be like flint in my determination to obey my Father God and receive His approval no matter what the world might say about me or do to me.

Beloved we are told to let this mind be in us (Philippians 2:5). Will we? When we receive by faith, this mind of Christ, the power of the Lamb Himself will overtake and consume us and the hidden areas of darkness and self-centeredness will be devoured by the flaming Fire Himself. Trust him completely to take over your heart and live His very own life inside of you, my dear brother and sister. Now is the time for the glory of the Lamb to shine brightly and totally within the hearts of a prepared Bride (2 Peter 1:19).

FRUIT: MAKES A NAME FOR SELF, LIVES
FOR HIS OWN IMAGE AND REPUTATION

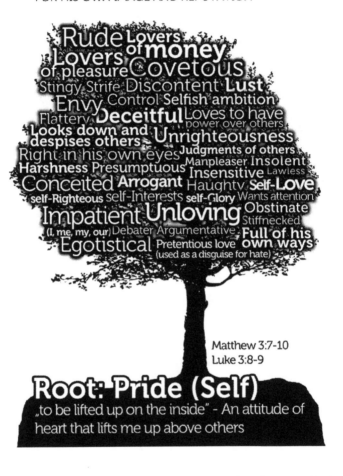

Rude Lovers of money
Lovers of pleasure Covetous
Stingy Strife Discontent Lust
Envy Control Selfish ambition
Flattery Deceitful Loves to have power over others
Looks down and despises others Unrighteousness
Right in his own eyes Judgments of others
Harshness Presumptuous Manpleaser Insolent Insensitive Lawless
Conceited Arrogant Haughty Self-Love
self-Righteous Self-Interests self-Glory Wants attention
Impatient Unloving Obstinate Stiffnecked
(I, me, my, our) Debater Argumentative Full of his
Egotistical Pretentious love own ways
(used as a disguise for hate)

Matthew 3:7-10
Luke 3:8-9

Root: Pride (Self)
„to be lifted up on the inside" - An attitude of
heart that lifts me up above others

*"Beware of false prophets who come to you in sheep's clothing but inwardly they are
ravenous wolves. You will know them by their fruits. Do men gather grapes from thorn
bushes or thigs from thistles? Even so, every good tree bears good fruit but a bad tree bears
bad fruit. Every tree that does not bear good fruit is cut down and thrown in to the fire.
Therefore, by their fruits you will know them"*

Matthew 7:15-20

FRUIT: A REVELATION OF THE SON OF GOD AND THE IMAGE OF CHRIST IS SEEN IN THE WORLD.

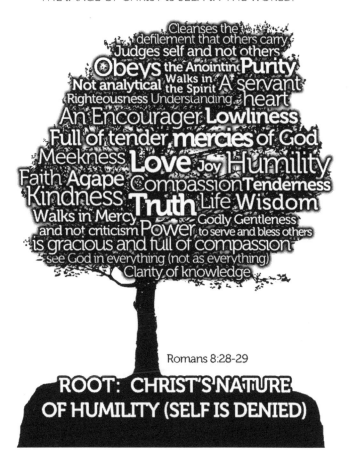

Cleanses the defilement that others carry. Judges self and not others. Obeys the Anointing Purity. Not analytical Walks in the Spirit A servant. Righteousness Understanding heart. An Encourager Lowliness. Full of tender mercies of God. Meekness Love Joy Humility. Faith Agape Compassion Tenderness. Kindness Truth Life Wisdom. Walks in Mercy and not criticism Power Godly Gentleness to serve and bless others. is gracious and full of compassion. see God in everything (not as everything). Clarity of knowledge.

Romans 8:28-29

ROOT: CHRIST'S NATURE OF HUMILITY (SELF IS DENIED)

"Beware of false prophets who come to you in sheep's clothing but inwardly they are ravenous wolves. You will know them by their fruits. Do men gather grapes from thorn bushes or thigs from thistles? Even so, every good tree bears good fruit but a bad tree bears bad fruit. Every tree that does not bear good fruit is cut down and thrown in to the fire. Therefore, by their fruits you will know them"

Matthew 7:15-20

The Hidden Secret

Before the Foundation of the world, father God had a wonderful plan. Even before He made man, he had an eternal purpose to fulfill. Sin did not alter or change his greatest of all plans. Paul called this the hidden wisdom of God which he concealed in a mystery before the world began.

"But, we speak the wisdom of God in a mystery, even the hidden wisdom, which God ordained before the world unto our glory."

1 Corinthians 2:7

"According as he hath chosen us in him before the foundation of the world, that we should be holy and without blame before him in love."

Ephesians 1:4

Father had a plan to have a family of sons and daughters and his family would bring great praise to the glory of his grace (Ephesians 1:5-6). This has all been planned by one heavenly Father before He even created anyone or anything on earth. In verse 9 Paul says, *"having made known unto us the mystery of his will, according to his good pleasure which he hath purposed in himself."* (Ephesians 1:1-9). All of this eternal plan was purposed, and imagined in himself. No angel, no other being, only the

Triune God knew about this wonderful mysterious, hidden plan! (Ephesians 1:10-11).

Scriptural verses that describe the Father's mystery hidden in himself:

"How that by revelation he made known unto me the mystery; (as I wrote afore in few words), Whereby, when ye read, ye may understand my knowledge in the mystery of Christ. Which in other ages was not made known unto the sons of men, as it is now revealed unto his holy apostles and prophets by the Spirit;"

Ephesians 3:3-5

"And to make all men see what is the fellowship of the mystery, which from the beginning of the world hath been hid in God, who created all things by Jesus Christ: To the intent that now unto the principalities and powers in heavenly places might be known by the church the manifold wisdom of God, According to the eternal purpose which he purposed in Christ Jesus our Lord."

Ephesians 3:9-11

"Now to him that is of power to establish you according to my gospel, and the preaching of Jesus Christ, according to the revelation of the mystery, which was kept secret since the world began, But now is made manifest, and by the scriptures of the prophets, according to the commandment of the everlasting God, made known to all nations for the obedience of faith"

Romans 16:25-26

"Whereof I am made a minister, according to the dispensation of God which is given to me for you, to fulfill the word of God; Even the mystery which hath been hid from ages and from generations, but now is made manifest to his saints: To whom God would make known what is the riches of the glory of this mystery among the Gentiles; which is Christ in you, the hope of glory"

Colossians 1:25-27

"That their hearts might be comforted, being knit together in love, and unto all riches of the full assurance of understanding, to the acknowledgement of the mystery of God, and of the Father, and of Christ; In whom are hid all the treasures of wisdom and knowledge."

Colossians 2:2-3

"But we speak the wisdom of God in a mystery, even the hidden wisdom, which God ordained before the world unto our glory"

1 Corinthians 2:7

The following phrases are some of the different ways to express this mystery before the foundation of the world:

"To fulfill the word of God" (Colossians 1:25b)
"Even the mystery which has been hid from ages." (Colossians 1-26a)
"the mystery." (Ephesians 3:3b)
"fellowship of the mystery" (Ephesians 3:9a)
"the eternal purpose." (Ephesians 3:11a)
"the hidden wisdom" (I Corinthians 2:7a)
"the revelation of the mystery." (Romans 16:25)

The very nature of God is all goodness, light, love, purity and perfection. The entire essence of God's being in total perfection. Therefore, since all beauty is contained within God; every good and beautiful thing comes from the Father of lights (James 1:17). It gives great joy for our heavenly father to reveal himself to his creation, because there is nothing good outside of Him. Every trace of goodness is coming out of His very nature.

As it was in the beginning

It has always been the plan of our Creator to reveal His very own perfect image within those he has created. In the very beginning was the wisdom of God. The wisdom of God comes out of His very heart and it is a complete, accurate revelation of his will, his way, and what pleases Him. All of his eternal wisdom has been poured into his eternal Word.

"In the beginning was the Word and the Word was with God and the Word was God."

John 1:1

One day the Word became flesh and dwelt amongst us.

"And the Word was made flesh, and dwelt among us, and we beheld his glory, the glory as of the only begotten of the Father, full of grace and truth"

John 1:14

From the very beginning, even before man was created, God desired to reveal His Wisdom in a person. A man that would show all of His image and rule his earth. Jesus taught his children to pray, *"Thy will be done, thy kingdom come on earth.*" (Matthew 6:10). We are called to *reign* in life through one, Jesus Christ (Roman 5:17).

To reveal and to rule

How are we to reveal God's heart and rule God's earth? A priest is to reveal the heart of God to his creation and a King is to rule God's domain.

> *"The earth is the Lord's and the fullness thereof."*
>
> (Psalm 24:1)

> *"All the ends of the world shall remember and turn unto the Lord: and all the kindreds of the nations shall worship before thee. For the kingdom is the Lord's: and he is the governor among the nation."*
>
> Psalm 22:27-28

Jesus told his disciples that all power and authority has been given to him, therefore go and teach all nations to observe all things that I taught you and I will be with you always (Matthew 28:18-20). One of the main things that Jesus taught them was to go everywhere proclaiming His Kingdom. In Psalm 2, we find the Father telling his Son to ask for the nations and surely He will give *all* nations as his *inheritance* to possess them as their Sovereign Lord. Jesus said whatever we ask in his name, he will do it. The body of Christ is a part of Christ and therefore they are to inherit what Christ has inherited (Romans 8:17).Some of the things that Christ has inherited are: All nations (Psalm 2:8) A more excellent name than any angel (Hebrews 1:4) and *all* things (Hebrews 1:2). What a glorious inheritance the body of Christ has in Him! No wonder Paul wrote that the eyes of our heart would be flooded with light to see the riches of the glory of his inheritance *in* the saints. (Ephesians 1:18). The entire body of Christ has a calling to be a priest and a King to God the Father in this world.

"And hath made us kings and priests unto God and his Father; to him be glory and dominion for ever and ever. Amen."

(Revelation 1:6)

What is the main power that God uses to cause us to reign *in* life through Jesus Christ? The answer is his eternal *wisdom*. In the very beginning was *the Word* and in the very beginning was *wisdom*. Proverbs chapter 8 is all about wisdom and many times it refers to wisdom as "someone". Wisdom has a mouth (Proverbs 8:4). Wisdom says, *"counsel is mine, and sound wisdom: I am understanding; I have strength. By Me kings reign, and princes decree justice. By me princes rule, and nobles, even all the judges of the earth"* (Proverbs 8:14-16).

The entire eighth chapter of Proverbs is filled with the excellence, the treasures and importance of *wisdom*. Verses 30 and 31 of Proverbs 8 are extremely relevant. *"Then I was by him: and I was as one brought up with him: and I was daily his delight, rejoicing always before him; Rejoicing in the habitable part of his earth; and my delights were with the sons of men."* Wisdom is here described as a Personality that has been in the very presence of God from the very beginning and always rejoicing in the Creator's handiwork.

It is through *wisdom* that kings reign! *"Wisdom hath builded her house, she hath hewn out her seven pillars"* (Proverbs 9:1). It is quite possible that the seven pillars of the house that wisdom is building are the seven spirits of God sent out into all the earth (Revelation 5:6). These seven spirits are coming out of the mind of the slain Lamb. In Philippians 2:5 we are commanded, *"to let this mind be in you, which was also in Christ Jesus."*

In Revelation chapter 17 we read about *"the mind which hath wisdom"* (vs. 9a). In the same chapter we also read about rulers of this earth that have "one mind" to make war with the Lamb (V. 13-14). In Colossians 2:2-3, we read of the mystery of God, being Christ *"in whom are hid all the treasures of wisdom and knowledge"*.

Within the eternal Word is hidden *all* the treasures of God's eternal wisdom. God has deposited all of his wisdom within the very being of his Word. God's eternal *wisdom* reveals God's *Word*, *Way* and *Will*. *"In him dwelleth all the fullness of the Godhead bodily."* (Colossians 2:9)

God's Original Plan

God desires to fill a man with his wisdom and through this eternal wisdom to reveal his heart and enable the man to rule in His stead. God's wisdom reveals God's heart and releases his authority. As the Word of God comes into fullness, then God's way, heart, mind and wisdom will be seen within a corporate body: This will then release the revelation of Christ in his body, which is the hidden mystery that has been buried in the heart of the Father before the foundation of the world.

"Who now rejoice in my sufferings for you, and fill up that which is behind of the afflictions of Christ in my flesh for his body's sake, which is the church: Whereof I am made a minister, according to the dispensation of God which is given to me for you, to fulfil the word of God; Even the mystery which hath been hid from ages and from generations, but now is made manifest to his saints: To whom God would make known what is the riches of the glory of this mystery among the Gentiles; which is Christ in you, the hope of glory."

(Colossians 1:24-27)

Once the Seed (Christ) has gone into the ground and died, it then could release this eternal hidden wisdom throughout the entire earth.

"But we speak the wisdom of God in a mystery, even the hidden wisdom, which God ordained before the world unto our glory: Which none of the princes of this world knew: for had they known it, they would not have crucified the Lord of glory."

1 Corinthians 2:7-8

When certain Greeks came to see Jesus, they were told by Jesus that the Seed had to go into the earth and die first. After the death of the Seed, now the risen Christ will bring forth much fruit in his disciples throughout the earth (John 12:24-26). John said that this Seed is living within the believer and "He" cannot sin (I John 3:9). This is the Seed that has crushed the serpent´s head (Genesis 3:15). This Seed sown into a heart becomes the true life of a believer.

God's original plan thwarted

Before the creation of man, a perverted form of wisdom came into the earth. Lucifer was created full of the wisdom of God. In the book of Ezekiel, the "prince" of Tyrus refers to the earthly ruler and the "king" of Tyrus refers to the spiritual ruler, being the devil.

*"Son of man, take up a lamentation upon the king of Tyrus, and say unto him, Thus saith the Lord God; Thou sealest up the sum, " **full of wisdom**", and perfect in beauty. Thou hast been in Eden the garden of God; every precious stone was thy covering, the sardius, topaz, and the diamond, the beryl, the onyx, and the jasper, the sapphire, the emerald, and the carbuncle, and gold: the workmanship of thy tabrets and of thy*

pipes was prepared in thee in the day that thou wast created. Thou art the anointed cherub that covereth; and I have set thee so: thou wast upon the holy mountain of God; thou hast walked up and down in the midst of the stones of fire. Thou wast perfect in thy ways from the day that thou wast created, till iniquity was found in thee."

Ezekiel 28:12-15

This is a thorough description of how the Creator made this tremendous anointed cherub. First, it is discovered that God is Lucifer's maker, apart from his Creator, he is nothing. God was the source of all that Lucifer had (vs. 14-15). Secondly, God made him perfect in all his ways (vs. 15). Thirdly, God made this cherub with a covering that consisted of every single precious stone in all of creation. This would mean that literally thousands of precious, colored gems covered Lucifer's being. These precious stones have no glory or radiance without the proper light. Fourthly, with the proper light, these stones would magnify the brilliance of the Light and the light would reflect "off" the stones at a much brighter radiance then how it entered "into" the stones. Lastly, all of the beauty, glory, brilliance that Lucifer had was only a reflection of *"Another".* None of it was his *own*: it *all* belonged to God; his Maker.

Whenever a heart sees itself as "special", "beautiful", or "gifted" *apart* from God's direct activity, this will result in an independent self-exalting poisonous attitude. It is his brilliance in us that causes us to shine. Jesus said that, *"apart from me you can do **nothing"** (John 15:5b).

This self-exalting attitude inside of the heart is *original sin.* Once the heart exalts itself, then it will start to speak evil of others and it will find fault with them. *Out of the abundance of the heart, the mouth will speak* (Matthew 12:34b).

Lucifer was created perfect until iniquity was found in him (Ezekiel 28:15). Lucifer's iniquity was a heart that rejoiced in its "own" beauty, splendor and goodness and therefore he became an independent entity that could only see its own worth! This independent heart that is lifted up sees others as a threat to its own glory and majesty!

Lucifer's heart was filled with violence because of the multitude of his merchandise. What is this merchandise? This merchandise was information that he sold to others. One of the meanings for this word merchandiser is tale-bearer. God says that there shall not be a tale-bearer amongst his people. This is referred to as an evil tongue. Lucifer sold information about God to the other angels. Lucifer will sell his merchandise (information) to anyone that will buy from him.

When someone receives the devil's merchandise, his heart is then filled with violence. If I receive demonic merchandise about myself, then I will start to hate myself. If I receive demonic merchandise about others; then I will start to hate others. If I receive demonic merchandise (information) about God, then I will start to hate and blame God.

"By the multitude of thy merchandise they have filled the midst of thee with violence, and thou hast sinned: therefore I will cast thee as profane out of the mountain of God: and I will destroy thee, O covering cherub, from the midst of the stones of fire."

Ezekiel 28:16

"The earth also was corrupt before God, and the earth was filled with violence."

Genesis 6:11

When someone receives the devil's merchandise, then violent thoughts start to enter their heart. Peter and David referred to this as an evil tongue. If I don't put away from me this evil tongue, then I will not be blessed and I will not be a blessing to others (see Psalm 34:11-14 and 1

Peter 3:8-11). We read in Genesis chapter 6 that people's minds were filled with evil thoughts and then the whole earth was filled with violence. This is the work of the merchandiser! Satan's extreme beauty and brightness caused his heart to be filled with pride and the wisdom that was in him to be perverted and destroyed.

"Thine heart was lifted up because of thy beauty, thou hast corrupted thy wisdom by reason of thy brightness: I will cast thee to the ground, I will lay thee before kings, that they may behold thee"

Ezekiel 28:17

This was the beginning of another wisdom. No longer was the pure wisdom of God, which is full of humility seen on earth, but now it was a demonic, selfish, defiled wisdom!

This pure eternal wisdom that reveals the heart and nature of God to his creation was replaced by a demonic self-centred wisdom that reveals the heart of satan to mankind.

Whose Image and Which Mind

"And as we have born the image of the earthly, so let us also bear the image of the heavenly"

1 Corinthians 15:49, literal meaning

"Here is the mind that has wisdom"

Revelation17:9a

God desired His image to be seen through mankind revealing His wisdom. But, man lost the image of God after the fall. Man's nature now became a distorted image of the true image of the Creator. Adam had a son in his own image and not the true image of God (Genesis 5:3). Man's wisdom was no longer a reflection of God's heart. Now, the wisdom of man became a reflection of satan's selfish heart. This is referred to in the book of Proverbs as foolishness.

In Prov. 22:15a it says that foolishness is bound in the heart of every child and this is why they need correction. God's plan to reveal *His wisdom, His word* and *His way* was thwarted by Satan's plan to reveal his wisdom, his words and his ways. There are clearly two different forms of wisdom on the earth today and every Christian can operate in an earthly or heavenly wisdom.

"And the tongue is a fire, a world of iniquity: so is the tongue among our members, that it defileth the whole body, and setteth on fire the course of nature; and it is set on fire of hell. For every kind of beasts, and of birds, and of serpents, and of things in the sea, is tamed, and hath been tamed of mankind: But the tongue can no man tame; it is an unruly evil, full of deadly poison. Therewith bless we God, even the Father; and therewith curse we men, which are made after the similitude of God. Out of the same mouth proceedeth blessing and cursing. My brethren, these things ought not so to be. Doth a fountain send forth at the same place sweet water and bitter? Can the fig tree, my brethren, bear olive berries? Either a vine, figs? so can no fountain both yield salt water and fresh. Who is a wise man and endued with knowledge among you? let him shew out of a good conversation his works with meekness of wisdom. But if ye have bitter envying and strife in your hearts, glory not, and lie not against the truth. This wisdom descendeth not from above, but is earthly, sensual, devilish. For where envying and strife is, there is confusion and every evil work. But the wisdom that is from above is first pure, then peaceable, gentle, and easy to be entreated, full of mercy and good fruits, without partiality, and without hypocrisy. And the fruit of righteousness is sown in peace of them that make peace."

James 3:6-18

This passage of scripture reveals that if there is earthly, demonic wisdom in the heart of a Christian, then it will come out of their thoughts, words and actions. Verse 13 says that the one who is full of God's heavenly wisdom will demonstrate this by a lifestyle of meekness, which is the true sign of wisdom. The next verse (vs.14) says, *"but if ye have bitter envy and strife in your hearts, glory not and don't lie against the truth."* These are three important words: bitter (bitterness) envy (envy) and strife (selfish ambition or a desire for others to honor you). This word for strife is *eritheia* (G2052) in strong's concordance. It means a selfish ambition, a desire to put oneself forward. It is contention, electioneering or intriguing for office, a partisan spirit. This same word was found before New Testament times where it denotes "a self-seeking pursuit of political office by unfair means." The person with this in their heart might speak the "right" things, but in their spirit is contention, strife and they are trying to get the vote of the listeners. Paul says in Philippians 1:15 that, *"some indeed preach Christ even of envy and strife and some also of good will."* This means that some preachers were preaching Jesus with their mouth, but in their heart they were really trying to project their own image and to promote themselves. Therefore, James says if this selfish ambition is in the heart of a Christian then they should not rejoice and not lie against the truth (James 3:14). Because this wisdom in them does not come down from above, but is earthly, sensual and devilish (James 3:15). This is the perverted wisdom that comes from the heart of Satan. This hidden demonic wisdom creates envy and strife and wherever this wisdom is found, there is confusion and every evil thing (James 3:16).

"But the wisdom that is from above is first pure, then peaceable, gentle, easy to be entreated, full of mercy and good fruits."

(James 3:17a)

The scriptures make a clear distinction between worldly, demonic wisdom and heavenly pure, wisdom.

Two kinds of wisdom

The proud, self-exalting heart of the evil one and the lowly, submissive heart of the lowly One each release wisdom. The proud, self-exalted heart of satan is full of this worldly corrupted wisdom. The lowly, self-denying heart of the Lamb of God is full of heavenly, pure, eternal wisdom.

In the Bible there is no clarification as to which wisdom it is referring to. One must know by the spirit whether it is the corrupted wisdom or the heavenly wisdom. God says to Jeremiah, "What wisdom is in them?" (Jeremiah 8:9). The people of God were living in a demonic, worldly wisdom that rejected the word of the Lord.

Phrases that describe demonic, corrupted wisdom:

Wisdom of this world (1 Cor. 3:19)

Fleshly wisdom (2 Cor. 1:12)

Thine own wisdom (Prov.23:4)

Corrupted wisdom (Ezek. 28:17)

Foolishness (Proverbs)

Wisdom of the wise (1 Cor. 1:19)

Phrases that describe heavenly wisdom:

Wisdom from above (James 3:17)

Wisdom of God (1 Cor.2:7a)

Wisdom (does not state which wisdom, it depends on the context)

Meekness; the true wisdom (James 3:13)

Fear of the Lord (Prov. 9:10, Job 28:28)

Hidden wisdom (Job 28:21, 1Cor. 2:7)

There is a wisdom that is not of this world and there is a wisdom that is totally of this world. The wisdom of this world is rooted in learning the ways of this world system. This wisdom began with Lucifer deceiving Adam and Eve into eating the forbidden fruit of the tree of knowledge of good and evil. Jesus said that every tree must bear fruit after its very own kind. Every tree is known by the fruit that it produces. Therefore, when man ate from the forbidden tree, he received the fruit of a corrupted demonic wisdom. The corrupted wisdom caused him to believe that he was wise. The truth was that his proud, selfish heart, now believed the demonic lie that he was always right and his way was the only way on earth! *"And when the woman saw that the tree was good for food, and that it was pleasant to the eyes, and a tree to be desired to make one "wise."* (Gen. 3:6a). She was enticed to eat from the tree so that she could be wise. This is how this demonic, corrupted wisdom of satan got inside of the heart of mankind. We also read in Proverbs 3:7a *"be not wise in thine own eyes: fear the Lord, and depart from evil"* and *"the way of a fool is right in his own eyes"* (Prov. 12:15a).

The fruit of the forbidden tree

Once man disobeyed God and ate from the forbidden tree, he became wise in his own eyes with a selfish demonic corrupted wisdom. This produced the fruit of pride which convinced mankind that all of "their" ways are always right. *"All the ways of a man are clean in his own eyes."* (Prov. 16:2a) and *"every way of a man is right in his own eyes."* (Prov. 21:2a).

This fruit is the very same fruit that entered Satan's heart when he allowed iniquity to be formed in him. He believed that his brightness, (which was *only* a reflection of God's glory) belonged to himself and he was the source of it. *"Thine heart was lifted up because of thy beauty, thou hast corrupted thy wisdom by reason of thy brightness."* (Ezek. 28:17a). Every tree must bear fruit after its own kind. So, God's greatest creation (mankind) lost their way, which was to live in the Presence of God and eat from the tree of life and dwell in His heart of wisdom. They now entered into another path and they got off the ancient path of the heart of Father God. Therefore, God told his prophet Jeremiah to call his people back to the ancient pathway. Thus says the Lord, *"Stand by the ways and see and ask for the ancient paths, Where the good way is, and walk in it; And you will find rest for your souls. But they said, 'We will not walk in it'"* (Jer. 6:16).

"Because my people hath forgotten me, they have burned incense to vanity, and they have caused them to stumble in their ways from the ancient paths, to walk in paths, in a way not cast up; To make their land desolate, and a perpetual hissing."

Jeremiah 18:15,16a

The apostle Paul said the same thing in Romans, that all men have gotten out of the way and there is not one single person that does good (Romans 3:10, 12).

This ancient way is the good way and it leads to finding rest for one's soul! We read in Matthew 11:29, *"Take my yoke upon you, and learn of me; for I am meek and lowly in heart: and ye shall find rest unto your souls."* Jesus is the good way; He is the ancient Path straight into the Father's heart. *"I am the Way, the Truth, and the Life."* (John 14:6a).

When someone takes the yoke of humility, which is the heart of the slain Lamb, they will then find the ancient path into the very heart of the heavenly Father. Living in Father's heart is the same as living in the eternal Wisdom of God.

If the rulers of this world system would have known this, they would not have crucified the Lord of glory (1 Cor. 2:8). Wisdom was in the beginning, with God and the Word was in the beginning with God. (John 1, Proverbs 8). God´s eternal plan was connected to his lovely, eternal Word and eternal Wisdom.

In Job 28 it is revealed that there is a place where even gold is refined. This is the secret place of the Most High (Ps. 91). There is a way that leads to this place in God. *"God understandeth the way thereof, and he knoweth the place thereof."* (Job 28:23) The ancient path leads to this place in the heart of God. But, in Job 28:7, 8 we read that this path *"cannot be known by birds of prey, and the falcon´s eye has not seen it. The proud beasts (and their young) have not trodden it, nor has the fierce lion passed over it."*

Until a person deals with his critical eye that looks for death and his evil proud, angry heart; he will not be allowed to see the ancient path to this secret place in God. In this place, there is wisdom, there is the heart of the Father, there is deep refining of the heart and there is tremendous glory and safety. Job asks, *"where shall wisdom be found?* (Job 28:12) *It is not in the land of the living* (vs. 13) *Where then cometh wisdom? And where is the place of understanding?* (vs. 20) *Seeing it is hid from the eyes of the living* (vs. 21a) *God understands the way thereof, and he knoweth the place thereof*" (vs. 23).

Wisdom can only be found in the heart of God. The wisdom that is found on earth is another kind of wisdom. It is the "Ancient path" that leads to this place of eternal, heavenly wisdom. David said, *"See if there be any wicked way in me, and lead me in the way everlasting"* (Psalm 139:24). The word that David used for the way everlasting is the same word for the ancient pathway! David was asking the Lord to search him deeply and see if there was a hurtful, painful wicked way inside of his heart. Once the wicked, hurtful way is discovered, then he wanted the Lord to put him back on the ancient way. God said David is a man after my own heart (Acts 13:22). David wanted his heart to please God, especially in his thoughts and meditations (Psalm 19:14, Psalm 139:23, 24).

The Holy Spirit is preparing a Bride for the Son and she will be one with the heart of the Lamb, this is why she is called the Lamb's wife.

Earthly, sensual and devilish wisdom or heavenly, eternal wisdom

What are the characteristics of these two types of wisdom? Earthly, demonic wisdom relies upon enticing words that *men* speak to cause change.

"And I, brethren, when I came to you, came not with excellency of speech or of wisdom, declaring unto you the testimony of God. For I determined not to know anything among you, save Jesus Christ, and him crucified. And I was with you in weakness, and in fear, and in much trembling.

And my speech and my preaching was not with enticing words of man's wisdom, but in demonstration of the Spirit and of power."

1 Corinthians 2:1-4

Heavenly wisdom relies on the Presence of the Living Word to cause change (1 Cor. 2:4-8, 13, Acts 12:24, James 3:13, 1 John 1:1-3 and Eph. 3:9-11). Earthly, demonic wisdom tries to create unity and peace. The heavenly wisdom speaks out of a heart of unity and releases the seed of peace to those who want peace (James 3:13-18). Earthly, demonic wisdom has an ulterior motive hidden in their heart (James 3:14). Heavenly wisdom is pure and then peaceable and only seeks to exalt God (James 3:17). Earthly, demonic wisdom appears to preach Christ and goodness, but in reality it is only concerned about how others think about them (Phil. 1: 15-18). Heavenly wisdom can appear offensive to people, but it is really the offense of the cross, which is the wisdom of God that is offending people (1 Cor. 1 and 2, Gal. 6:12-14). Earthly, demonic wisdom focuses on externals such as speech, while heavenly wisdom focuses on revealing the lowly heart of the Lamb (Matt 11:25-29, James 3:13). Earthly, demonic wisdom is hindered from receiving divine revelation (Matt. 11:25). Heavenly wisdom receives great revelation because it takes the lowly place of a child and does not depend on its own ability at all (Matt. 11:25-26, 1 Cor. 2:3,4; 2 Cor. 12:9,10). Lastly, earthly wisdom is coming to a final end (1. Cor. 1:19). Heavenly wisdom will rule and reign throughout the entire kingdom of our glorious King forever.

Father God's ultimate plan of restoration

For ages there has been a mystery hidden deep within the bosom of God. (John 1:18) The apostle Paul carried a great burden to see the fulfillment of this eternal mystery of the Father; which is the revelation of his image in His Son (Rom. 8:28, 29).

"For I want you to know how great is my solicitude for you [how severe an inward struggle I am engaged in for you] and for those [believers] at Laodicea, and for all who [like yourselves] have never seen my face and known me personally. [For my concern is] that their hearts may be braced (comforted, cheered, and encouraged) as they are knit together in love, that they may come to have all the abounding wealth and blessings of assured conviction of understanding, and that they may become progressively more intimately acquainted with and may know more definitely and accurately and thoroughly that mystic secret of God, [which is] Christ (the Anointed One).3 In Him all the treasures of [divine] wisdom (comprehensive insight into the ways and purposes of God) and [all the riches of spiritual] knowledge and enlightenment are stored up and lie hidden."

Colossians 2:1-3, Amplified Bible

In Christ are hidden all the treasures of eternal wisdom. When a person is allowed to behold the beautiful face of Jesus Christ, they are beholding the glory of God in fullness! Col. 3:16a says, *"Let the Word of Christ dwell in you in all wisdom."* This is the Living Word that forms the risen Christ and reveals the eternal wisdom of God in a mystery that has been hidden, but is now being revealed! This is not saying that we should memorize the scriptures. This is referring to the hidden wisdom that is being revealed in the living person called the Word of God (John 1:1-4). We read in Rev. 10:7 that the mystery of God shall be completed and brought to its full end. The fullness and completion of this eternal mystery will reveal the full glory of God's image within the body of Christ. All of creation has been groaning for this fullness to take place, when the Son is revealed within his body on earth (Rom. 8:17-19).

Paul labored with all of his strength to see Christ formed within a corporate body on earth (Col. 1:25-29). In verse 27, it says the mystery is Christ in you and "you" is in the plural. This means that the mystery is about Christ in a corporate body. There is no greater revelation and demonstration of the eternal heavenly wisdom of God than the cross. It is the cross that reveals wisdom from a heavenly perspective. Wisdom is not something, but Someone.

"But of him are ye in Christ Jesus, who of God is made unto us wisdom, and righteousness, and sanctification, and redemption"
1 Corinthians 1:30

Christ becomes wisdom for every believer. Man's wisdom is to display *his* power through *his* strength and force. The force of men is revealed through outward strength, but God's wisdom is revealed in weakness. The greatest victory was accomplished through a gentle, quiet helpless lamb. This is the wisdom of God. Father is waiting for the body of His Son on earth to let this same mind be in them that was in Christ 2000 years ago. It's now time for the church to demonstrate to the invisible principalities and powers the wisdom of God by walking in the heart of meekness!

"Whereby, when ye read, ye may understand my knowledge in the mystery of Christ, which in other ages was not made known unto the

*sons of men, as it is now revealed unto his holy apostles and prophets by the Spirit; That the Gentiles should be fellow heirs, and of the same body, and partakers of his promise in Christ by the gospel: Whereof I was made a minister, according to the gift of the grace of God given unto me by the effectual working of his power. Unto me, who am less than the least of all saints, is this grace given, that I should preach among the Gentiles the unsearchable riches of Christ; And to make all men see what is the fellowship of the mystery, which from the beginning of the world hath been hid in God, who created all things by Jesus Christ: To the intent that now unto the principalities and powers in heavenly places might be known **by the church** the manifold wisdom of God, according to the eternal purpose which he purposed in Christ Jesus our Lord."*

Ephesians 3:4-11

The world scorns weakness, but the Father God needs weakness, because He shows his eternal power in our weaknesses. The world is afraid of showing its weakness because it makes them look helpless and feel vulnerable. The apostle Paul prayed that the Lord would remove his thorn because it made him feel so uncomfortable. This thorn made Paul feel so very weak and dependent. Nobody wants to have a thorn in their flesh. It feels so much better to be strong and healthy in our bodies. We also as Paul would beg the Lord to remove this uncomfortable thorn from our flesh (2 Corinthians 12:7, 8). If we knew like Paul knew that this thorn was a messenger from satan to buffet us, then of course, it would be right to ask the Lord to remove it (vs. 7). Our natural mind would definitely assume that since this was a messenger of satan, then it is not to be tolerated by us! *What* the thorn was is not important, but *why* God allowed the thorn is very important!

The reason that the Lord allowed satan to buffet Paul with the thorn is to stop Paul from exalting himself. Heavenly wisdom **never** *exalts self*.

This is the hour for Father God to reveal to all the hosts of heaven His very own eternal wisdom. Heavenly wisdom is revealed in the weakness of a Lamb conquering all the hosts of hell and revealing the mind and heart of God. From the beginning of time, our heavenly father wanted his creation to realize that it is only in his lowly heart that we discover life and live as conquerors.

Summary

The hidden secret inside the very heart of God is his eternal wisdom revealed in his eternal Word. One day, this Wisdom became flesh and dwelt amongst us and demonstrated what was hidden in the Father´s heart. To see the Word is to see the hidden glory of God in the face of Jesus Christ. The Son of God living his life on earth is the full revelation of the eternal wisdom of God. Now, this Son has a body on earth and as they reveal the heart and mind of the Son, then the world and its rulers will see the wisdom and power of God. The eternal hidden mystery of God and Christ is about to come to fullness.

This is a day that all of creation has been longing for, because creation yearns to behold the majesty and wisdom of its Creator. Now is the time for a people on earth to show to all the invisible forces the glory and manifold wisdom of its God (Ephesians 3:10). It is only in the meek and lowly heart of God that his eternal wisdom and word can be understood. There is another demonic corrupted form of this eternal wisdom and it reveals the glory of men´s strength. But true wisdom reveals the glory of God in men´s weakness. He is our Strength and He is all that we need to experience the fullness of life in every degree. His strength is made perfect in our weakness (2 Corinthians 12:9). As the body of Christ refuses to fear their weakness and learns to rejoice in His strength, they can go up and down the earth proclaiming his victory! *"So, I will strengthen them in the Lord. And they shall walk up and down in His name says the Lord."*(Zechariah 10:12). His wisdom will be revealed by the revelation of his heart in this day. This is the hour for heavenly wisdom to be revealed by a heavenly Christ through a heavenly people on earth! As these heavenly ones walk in the lowly, pure love of the Lamb, the glory of God will come in its fullness!

A Closing Prayer

Father God, may your heart find complete satisfaction at this hour through your Son living his life through his corporate body on earth. May the church or the body of Christ reveal your wisdom by walking in humility. May the world behold your Lamb risen within a people and ruling on the throne of their hearts! Amen.

In the bond of Calvary's Love,
Greg Violi

Other books by Greg Violi

Depression and Introspection: Healing for the Diseased Mind:
The purpose of God in creation is to have a people live in His presence and to find joy, peace and love in Him. Often due to disappointments, troubles and difficulties, fear blocks individuals from living in the Presence of God. If Healing does not take place, these experiences will release a diseased way of thinking. People will actually create a presence of a wounded, fearful self in which to live their life instead of living in God's presence. This new booklet explains how to overcome these experiences and learn to live in the presence of God.

The Lamb's Heart
This is Greg's second book and is an in depth study of the heart with special emphasis on brokenness and the heart of the Lamb.

The Secrets of a Fantastic Marriage
This book reveals how to experience a fantastic marriage because it explains in an in-depth way how to live in the heart of God and to allow Christ to be formed within individuals.

For more information about Greg Violi, his ministry, itinerary, and materials visit the following websites:
→ *www.aplaceforhisglory.com*
→ *www.erweckt.de*

To contact or invite Greg Violi please use this link:
→ *http://gregvioli.startlogic.com/contact/*
You can also use this email: *kontakt@greg-violi.de*

89262227R00030

Made in the USA
Columbia, SC
20 February 2018